KT-430-289

One World

In the Country

Valerie Guin

W
FRANKLIN WATTS
LONDON•SYDNEY

Note
about the series
One World is designed to encourage young readers to find out more about people and places in the wider world. The photographs have been carefully selected to stimulate discussion and comparison.

First published in 2004 by Franklin Watts
96 Leonard Street, London EC2A 4XD

Franklin Watts Australia
45-51 Huntley Street, Alexandria, NSW 2015

© Franklin Watts 2004

Editor: Caryn Jenner
Designer: Louise Best
Art director: Jonathan Hair
Map: Ian Thompson
Reading consultant: Hilary Minns, Institute of Education, Warwick University

Acknowledgements: Tim Beddow/Hutchison: 18. Tony Binns/Easi-Images: 13. David Cummings/ Eye Ubiquitous: 24t. Mark Edwards/Still Pictures: 26. Sarah Errington/Hutchison: 3, 16. Robert Francis/Hutchison: 24b. Gallo Images/Eye Ubiquitous: 10. Patricio Goycoolea/ Hutchison: 12. Carlos Guarita/Still Pictures: 19. Jean Hall/Holt Studios: 20. Roger De La Harpe/ Gallo Images/ Corbis: 9. Juliet Highet/Hutchison: 15t. Jeremy Horner/Hutchison: 14. Wayne Hutchinson/Holt Studios: 11. L. Johnstone/Eye Ubiquitous: endpapers, 15b. P Karunakaran/Holt Studios: 23. Roy Maconachie/Easi-Images: 21. JC Moschetti/ Still Pictures: cover, 17b. Ray Pfortner/Still Pictures: 25. Bryan Pickering/Eye Ubiquitous: 6. Bill Ross/Corbis: 8. Sarah Rowland/Holt Studios: 22. Tony Souter/Hutchison: 7.

Every attempt has been made to clear copyright. Should there be any inadvertent omission, please apply to the publisher for rectification.

A CIP catalogue record for this book is available from the British Library

ISBN 0 7496 5442 2

All rights reserved. No part of this publication may be reproduced, stored in a retrieval system, or transmitted in any form or by any means, electronic, mechanical, photocopy, recording or otherwise, without the prior written permission of the copyright owner.

Printed in Malaysia

Contents

Our countryside 6

Natural places 8

Wild animals 10

Farm animals 12

Growing food 14

After the harvest 16

Village life 18

Country crafts 20

Special events 22

Enjoying the countryside 24

Saving the countryside 26

All around the world 28

Glossary and index 30

Our countryside

All around the world, there
is countryside. Countryside
is land that is away from
towns and cities.

This is a **map** of all the **countries** in the world. Read this book to find out about countryside all over the world.

This boy is walking in the countryside. In this book, you will see lots of different things in different kinds of countryside.

Natural places

In the countryside, there are **natural** things such as trees and other plants. Many trees grow in this **forest** in Canada. It is autumn, and the leaves on the trees are turning from green to gold and orange.

Brightly coloured wildflowers grow in this field in South Africa. These flowers are not planted by people. The seeds are scattered by animals and by the wind.

Wild animals

Different kinds of wild animals live in the countryside. This elephant family is feeding on the grass of the African **savannah** in Tanzania.

Rabbits live wild in many parts
of the world. In Sweden, there
are many fields and forests
where rabbits can hop about.

Farm animals

Some animals in the
countryside live on farms.
This farmer in Spain keeps
sheep for wool and meat.

In many places, such as China, farmers use water buffalo to help on farms. At the end of the day's work, the water buffalo cool off in the river.

Growing food

Many different kinds of **crops** are
grown on farms. These farm workers
in Vietnam are planting rice in a field
called a paddy. Rice is the most
common food in the world.

Crops need time to grow and become **ripe**, then they can be **harvested**. These workers in France are picking ripe grapes.

This machine cuts ripe wheat in a field in the Ukraine. Wheat is used to make bread and other foods.

After the harvest

Grassy plants that are used for food, such as wheat and rice, are called grain. These women in Sudan are separating out the part of the ripe grain that can be eaten. This is called winnowing.

These men in Chile are
putting ripe wheat into
a machine which
separates the grain.

Village life

A village is a small town in the countryside. On market day, people gather to buy and sell fruit and vegetables that they have grown. This is a village market in Belgium.

In some villages, people prepare their meals together. These women in Nigeria are peeling a vegetable called manioc. They are preparing enough food for several families.

Country crafts

People often use **materials** from the countryside to make things for the home. This woman in Ireland uses willow from nearby trees to weave baskets.

This woman in Bolivia weaves
wool into colourful cloth. The
wool comes from a large farm
animal called an alpaca.

Special events

At a country fair, there are shows and competitions for people living in the countryside. These horses are pulling a cart around the show ring at a country fair in Britain.

Many people watch the ox races that take place in country villages in southern India every summer.

Enjoying the countryside

These hikers are on a walking holiday in Peru, where there are well-marked mountain trails.

Campers have set up this tent on the side of a lake in Australia. The tent shelters the campers when they sleep outdoors.

This family in New Zealand have come to the countryside for a picnic. The boys are looking for fish and insects in the shallow river. They are being very careful, because they do not want to spoil the countryside.

Saving the countryside

The countryside must be protected to keep it natural. These children are picking up rubbish from a beach in the United States.

These children in Sri Lanka are on their way to plant new trees. The new trees will replace trees that have been chopped down.

All around the world

All around the world,
there is countryside.

Canada

United
States

Ireland
Britain
Spain

The countries that you
have read about are
shown in pink on this
map of the world. Find
the country that matches
each picture in the book.

Peru

Bolivia

Chile

Belgium

Ukraine

Sweden

France

China

India

Sri Lanka

Vietnam

Sudan

Tanzania

Nigeria

Australia

South
Africa

New
Zealand

Glossary

countries places with their own governments

crops plants grown for food

forest an area of land where lots of trees grow

harvest to pick ripe crops

map a drawing that shows where places are

materials things used to make other things

natural not made by people, but part of nature

ripe ready to be picked or eaten

savannah a grassy area of land in a hot place

Index

animals 9, 10, 12, 14, 16, 27

beach 26

campers 24
country fair 22
crops 14, 15

farms 12, 13, 14
field 9, 11, 14, 15
forest 8, 11

grain 16

harvest 15, 16
hikers 24

lake 24

market 18
mountain 24

ox races 23

paddy 14
picnic 25

plant 8, 9, 14, 16, 27

river 13, 25

savannah 10

trees 8, 20, 27

villages 18, 19

winnowing 16